by James Preller

SCHOLASTIC INC.

New York   Toronto   London   Auckland   Sydney

Exclusive worldwide licensing agent: Momentum Partners, Inc., New York, NY

Photo Credits:
front cover: (clockwise from top left) © Clay Myers/ The Wildlife Collection; © Bruce Rowell/Masterfile; © David T. Roberts, Natures Images, Inc./Photo Researchers, Inc.; ©1995 M H Sharp/Photo Researchers, Inc.; © 1996 Paragon Entertainment Corporation; © Robert Parks/The Wildlife Collection; © David Maitland/Masterfile; © 1996 Paragon Entertainment Corporation; Laura Wilkinson/ © 1996 Paragon Entertainment Corporation; © Comstock **back cover:** (center) Mark Tomalty/Masterfile (other photos) © 1996 Paragon Entertainment Corporation

p. 3: Laura Wilkinson/© 1996 Paragon Entertainment Corporation **p. 4:** © 1996 Paragon Entertainment Corporation **p. 5:** (clockwise from top left): © Rod Planck/Photo Researchers, Inc.; © John Foster/Masterfile; © Robert Parks/The Wildlife Collection **p. 6:** © 1996 Paragon Entertainment Corporation **p.7:** (clockwise from top left): © 1986 G.C. Kelley/Photo Researchers, Inc.; © Clay Myers/The Wildlife Collection; © 1994 Gregory G. Dimijian/Photo Researchers, Inc.; © Patti Murray/Animals Animals **p. 8:** © Scott Camazine **p. 9:** (left) © 1996 Paragon Entertainment Corporation; (right) Laura Wilkinson/ © 1996 Paragon Entertainment Corporation **p. 10:** © Breck P. Kent/Animals Animals **p. 11:** (clockwise from top left): © Animals Animals; © Patti Murray/Animals Animals; © Clay Myers/The Wildlife Collection **p. 12:** © 1996 Paragon Entertainment Corporation **p. 13:** (left) © Rod Planck/Photo Researchers, Inc.; (right) © David Maitland/Masterfile **p. 14:** (left) © Breck P. Kent/Animals Animals; (top right) © David T. Roberts, Nature's Images, Inc./Photo Researchers, Inc.; (bottom right) © Stephen Dalton/Photo Researchers, Inc. **p. 15:** (clockwise from top left) © John Foster/Masterfile; © Fred Whitehead/Animals Animals; Laura Wilkinson/© 1996 Paragon Entertainment Corporation; © 1996 Paragon Entertainment Corporation **p. 16:** © Rudolf Freund **p. 17:** (top) © 1996 Paragon Entertainment Corporation; (bottom) Laura Wilkinson/ © 1996 Paragon Entertainment Corporation **p. 18:** (clockwise from top left) C.W.Perkins/ © Animals Animals; © David T. Roberts/Photo Researchers, Inc.; © Clay Myers/ The Wildlife Collection; © M H Sharp/Photo Researchers, Inc. **p. 19:** © Patti Murray/Animals Animals **p. 20:** (top) © G.J. Bernard/Animals Animals; (bottom) © Clay Myers/The Wildlife Collection **p. 21:** © 1977 D. Zielinski/Photo Researchers, Inc. **p. 22:** © Tim Laman/The Wildlife Collection **p. 23:** (top) © Michael Lustbader/Photo Researchers, Inc.; (bottom) © 1996 Paragon Entertainment Corporation **p. 24:** (top) Laura Wilkinson/© 1996 Paragon Entertainment Corporation; (bottom) © 1996 Paragon Entertainment Corporation **p. 25:** (clockwise from top left): Laura Wilkinson/© 1996 Paragon Entertainment Corporation; © 1996 Paragon Entertainment Corporation; Laura Wilkinson/Paragon Entertainment Corporation **p. 26:** (left) © 1996 Paragon Entertainment Corporation; (right) © Clay Myers/The Wildlife Collection **p. 27:** (all photos) © Clay Myers/The Wildlife Collection **p. 28:** Laura Wilkinson/© 1996 Paragon Entertainment Corporation **p. 29:** (top) K.H. Switak/Photo Researchers, Inc.; (bottom) © 1996 Paragon Entertainment Corporation **p. 30:** © 1996 Paragon Entertainment Corporation **p. 31:** (left) © 1996 Paragon Entertainment Corporation; (right) Laura Wilkinson/ © 1996 Paragon Entertainment Corporation **p. 32:** Laura Wilkinson/© 1996 Paragon Entertainment Corporation

No part of this publication may be reproduced in whole or in part, or stored in a retrieval system, or transmitted in any form or by any means electronic, mechanical, photocopying, recording, or otherwise, without written permission of the publisher. For information regarding permission, write to Scholastic Inc., 555 Broadway, New York, NY 10012.

ISBN 0-590-53742-3

Copyright © 1996 by Paragon Entertainment Corporation.
Kratts' Creatures ® and Ttark are registered trademarks of Paragon Entertainment Corporation.
All rights reserved. Published by Scholastic Inc.

Book design by Todd Lefelt

12 11 10 9 8 7 6 5 4 3 2 1   7 8 9/9 0 1 2/0

Printed in the U.S.A.
First Scholastic printing, April 1997

We love all kinds of creepy, crawly, wriggly, squiggly creatures that we call bugs. Living with them might bug some people, but not us.

Monarch Caterpillar

Dragonfly

Praying Mantis

We like to think of the world as one big, beautiful bug collection!

> Most bugs are insects, but... WHAT IS AN INSECT ANYWAY?

An insect is any one of those cool little creatures with bizarre shapes and weird features that crawl and fly around us. If it looks like a little alien from outer space, chances are you're looking at an insect from planet Earth.

But seriously, an insect usually has three pairs of legs, a segmented body, and two pairs of wings.

Insects have been living on Earth for at least 400 million years. And they have lived just about everywhere! They have survived in the hottest deserts, high in the mountains, deep in underground caves, even in the snow and ice of the Antarctic!

Giant Hairy Scorpion

Monarch Butterfly

Walking Stick

Pine White Butterfly

And there are a lot of them! Eighty-five percent of all living creatures are insects. In fact, there are more than 1,000,000 different species of insects alive today. And scientists are discovering new species all the time.

Fun Fact #1
Show a Cockroach Some Respect!

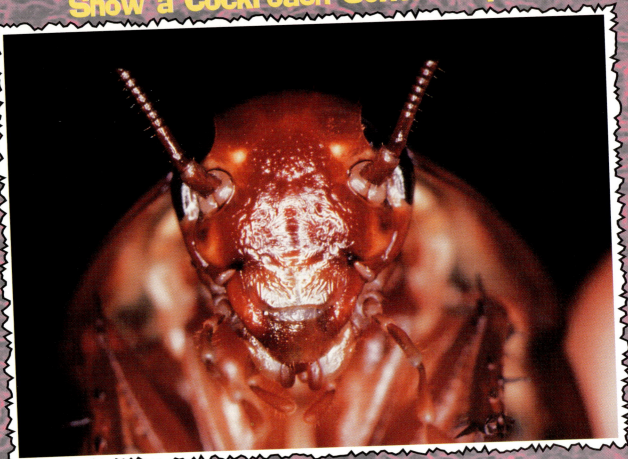

Talk about being around forever! According to fossils that scientists have found, these tough guys haven't changed in 250 million years. They've outlived the dinosaurs! If you ask us, cockroaches, and all other species of insects, deserve a little respect.

Creature Feature

Hi, guys! Allison here from the Creature Club. Speaking of cockroaches, there's one crawling on your head, Martin! It's a Madagascar hissing cockroach. This roach is no ordinary insect. His tiny brain is so advanced that he has his own cockroach language! The cockroach's language is made up of different hissing noises. For example, if a person picks him up, the cockroach hisses to say, "Let me go!"

Hey, I think this cockroach is trying to tell me my shampoo tastes good!

Let's look at the body of an insect. In this case, a butterfly.

HEAD
Antennae
Compound eye
Simple eye
Mouth parts

THORAX
Three pairs of legs
Wings

ABDOMEN
Spiracles (for breathing)

Of course there is no "typical insect." They come in all shapes and sizes. That's one of the things we love about them! Just look at all the different patterns and colors in these butterflies

Wood White Butterfly

Pine White Butterfly

Monarch Butterfly

Vinegaroon

**Butterflies have what it takes to be an insect.
If you'd like to be an insect, here's what you would need:**

1 A hard outer casing

2 Three body sections: the head, the thorax, and the abdomen

3 Almost all insects have wings, so you'll probably need them, too.

4 Three pairs of legs — a total of six. (There are some bugs in this book that you might think are insects, but aren't. They're arachnids. Keep your eye out for them, because if you step on one barefooted, it'll really let you know it!)

Hey, that vinegaroon we were looking at isn't an insect — it's one of those arachnids! We'll have more on those arachnids later!

Anyway, you know what it takes to be an insect. But did you know that some insects walk on walls and ceilings? Well, check out the fly! A fly has sticky pads on the ends of its feet.

Fly

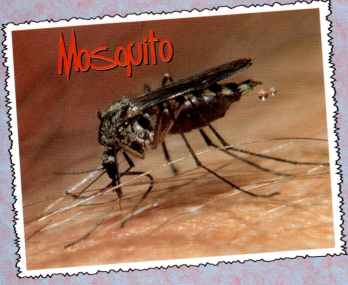

Mosquito

A fly, and other insects, can also taste things with its feet. That's why insect repellent works. When a mosquito lands on you, for example, it tastes so bad he just has to get outta there!

Imagine if you could taste ice cream by touching it with your feet!

Fun Fact #2
More Far-Out Facts About Insects' Feet and Legs

- A grasshopper can jump more than twenty times its own length. If you had that same super power, you could leap 80 feet in a single bound! And 80 feet is pretty long. It's almost as long as a basketball court!

- Crickets can hear with their front legs!

- Fleas have claws on the ends of their feet to give them a super grip. This helps them hold on to the hair of animals.

> **Now let's take a look at one insect's eyes.**

> **You'll see the most amazing thing....**

Most insects have two, large, compound eyes and three smaller, simpler eyes called ocelli. Of all the insects, the dragonfly has one of the best vision systems. Each compound eye is made up of thousands of tiny lenses. Each lens sees a small picture, like a piece of a jigsaw puzzle. We don't know what the world looks like to a dragonfly, but it must be pretty different from what we see. After all, our eyes have only one lens each.

Fun Fact #3

Army ants are on a constant quest for food. Millions of ants will march in a line, sometimes 300 feet long! What's amazing about this is they find their way by smell. They don't have eyes!

Yellow Jacket Wasp

Cricket

Some insects, such as female wasps and bees, sting. . . .

Some jump really far. . . .

Hercules Beetle

Monarch Butterfly

Others simply run away!

And here's a nifty trick. This monarch butterfly just tastes really, really bad.

Fun Fact #4

ATTENTION, BIRDS! DON'T EAT THIS GUY! HE'LL MAKE YOU SICK!

This monarch caterpillar is brightly colored. Rather than trying to hide, he wants birds to notice him. It's a warning, the caterpillar's way of saying: "Stay away! I taste gross!"

Monarch caterpillars eat the milkweed plant. Milkweed sap is poisonous to most animals, but not to the monarch caterpillar. However, if a bird tries to eat the caterpillar, which is full of milkweed poison (ptooey), it will vomit at once! And the same thing will happen when the caterpillar turns into a butterfly.

Insects are amazing for lots of other reasons, too. Here are some of the incredible things they do:

Water Strider

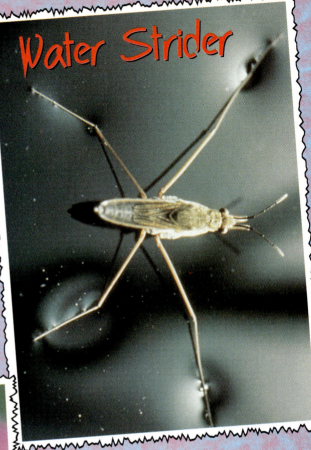

Some walk on water. . . .

Monarch Butterfly

Some fly thousands of miles. . . .

Some monarch butterflies spend the summer in North America and the winter in Mexico. The two-way flight averages 2,400 miles!

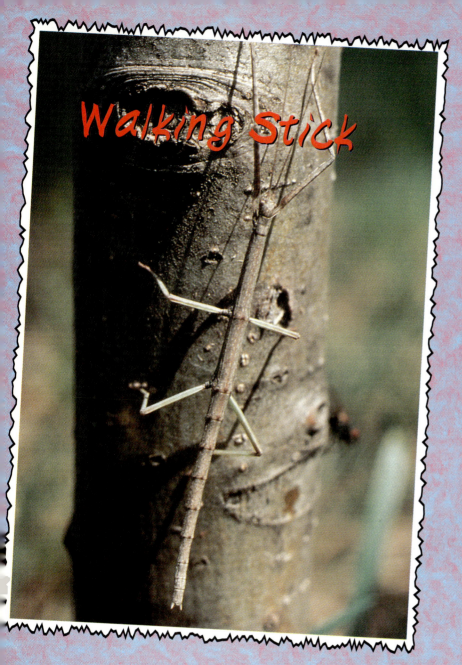

Walking Stick

Some are masters of disguise. . . .

Many insects are able to blend into their natural surroundings. This is called camouflage. Check out this stick insect. It looks like a twig from a tree. Other insects look like dead leaves, thorns, tree bark, even bird poop!

Ants Carrying a Millipede

Ten more pages until Ttark demonstrates the fabulous Dance of the Honeybee!

Besides just being cool, one of the reasons insects are so important is that they are food for other creatures. Birds, fish, frogs, bats, lizards, and other animals eat insects. Even insects eat insects!

Creature Feature

The Praying Mantis

Hey, guys, check out the praying mantis! She's a great example of an insect that eats other insects. The mantis is a predator. It's like the leopard of the insect world.

The praying mantis got her name because of the way she holds her two front legs. The mantis looks as though she is praying. But don't bet on it! Those front legs are poised — ready — to snatch a bug. The mantis doesn't chase her food. Instead she hides and waits for an insect to come by, then she strikes with lightning speed. Dinnertime!

Creature Feature

The Chilean Rose Tarantula

Hey, guys, I think I found one of those "non-insect" bugs. It's an arachnid called the Chilean rose tarantula. And it's crawling up your back, Martin! They are peaceful bugs but they have big sharp fangs. If you bug this tarantula, it can bite! The rose tarantula has other ways to defend herself, too. Her stomach is covered with urticating (ER-TI-KAY-TING), or stinging, hairs. If an enemy tries to bug her, she can detach these hairs and fling them like arrows!

Hey, where are you going?

"If you thought urticating was a big word, how about this one: metamorphosis!"

"Great word, Martin! Let's take a look at the amazing metamorphosis of the butterfly!"

Unlike humans, when butterflies and many other insects hatch, they look completely different from the way they look when they become adults. Let's look at the complete metamorphosis of the butterfly.

1 First the female butterfly lays her egg on a leaf.

Then:

Caterpillar

2 The egg hatches into a caterpillar, called a larva. The caterpillar eats a lot, molts, and grows.

3 The caterpillar clings to a branch or leaf. Its outside skin hardens to form a pupa, or chrysalis.

Pupa

Butterfly emerging from cocoon

4 Finally, the butterfly emerges . . . and flies away.

Psst! Here's another bug that isn't an insect . . . the scorpion.

Stinger

Emperor Scorpion

See that stinger on the tip of its tail? It's full of poison! That's why you don't want to step on this arachnid!

Creature Feature

Emperor Scorpion

Hey, what's all that white stuff on the scorpion's back? Those are baby scorpions! The mother carries them on her back and she protects them with her stinger.

But the emperor scorpion does not rule the forest. Baboons like to eat scorpions for a special treat; a hungry baboon will rip off the scorpion's tail and pop him right in his mouth, like a shrimp cocktail.

Fun Fact #5
Far-Out Facts About Spiders

- Most spiders use poison to kill or paralyze their prey.
- Most spiders have eight eyes — two rows of four each.
- There are 30,000 different species of spiders. Tarantulas are the biggest and black widows have the strongest poison.
- And remember, spiders are not insects, they're arachnids!

Sorry, we've run out of pages. So we won't be able to tell you any more really amazing, cool things about the world of bugs and insects.

But that doesn't mean you can't go hang out with a few of these cool creatures yourself.

"Hey, Chris, which bug is hairy and has a rose-colored abdomen?"

"The Chilean rose tarantula!"

"Right, and it just crawled onto your shoulder!"

"Cool! Bugs don't bug me!"

WARNING
DON'T TRY THIS AT HOME.